Your Magnificent Body

Health and Fitness for Pipeliners and Shiftworkers

Scarlet Knight

ISBN: 978-1-329-84802-3

Considering the Health Challenges Unique to the Shift Worker

Contents

Introduction

Shift work is demanding on your life, your family, and even your social life. It's especially demanding on your health. Whether you are a man or woman, working rotating shifts or night shifts, you may experience health and lifestyle challenges that the 9-5 worker does not know. To ignore the needs of the shift worker is irresponsible when you consider that health problems, deaths, and catastrophes such as the failure of the Space Shuttle Columbia and the crash of the Exxon Valdez have been attributed to human fatigue.

The variety of industries requiring around-the-clock staffing is vast. The Bureau of Labor Statistics reports that as many as 15 million Americans perform shift work. Casinos, hospitals, customer and communication service centers, and hospitality businesses employ staff on a 24/7 basis. Some industries that require shift work carry the weighty responsibility of providing for the health and safety of the public. These unique workers are faced with the challenge of working late into the night and early morning hours while maintaining watch over the well being of others. This list includes doctors, nurses, emergency response teams, pipeline control center personnel, transportation employees, law enforcement, and military personnel. Our society depends on these faithful and dedicated men and women who persevere through the night, keeping watch while most of us are sleeping.

The aim of this publication is to provide tools and guidelines for building healthier bodies. Improving your health will elevate your quality of life. A healthy employee is happier at home and on the job. Taking a strong, proactive approach to your health will make you more alert, improve your relationships, and reduce your sick days. Don't leave the health of your body to chance.

The nature of shift work increases the risk for physical and emotional complications. Working this type schedule disrupts your natural sleep patterns set by circadian rhythm. Some shift workers battle insomnia and depression. Studies have shown there is an increased risk of injuries and accidents for anyone, regardless of age or physical health, who is overly fatigued. Also, employees working rotating shifts have an increased risk of cardiovascular disease, gastrointestinal disease, and obesity.

This is not a hopeless situation! There are steps you can take and habits you can develop to alleviate the inherent risks associated with shift work. First, ask yourself if you have the desire for good health. Secondly, will you take action to make one change today that benefits your health? When you become comfortable with that one change, make one more and so on. Over time, you will develop a healthy habit or two. As you begin to enjoy the side effects of improved health, you will feel motivated to continue. Others will observe this new course in your life and ask questions. Get ready! They may even follow you in making changes of their own. This will eventually boost morale for everyone. It's never too late. Start today!

Your Magnificent Body

What a privilege to inhabit such a complex, capable body. There is no machine created by man that can parallel the vast list of amazing components that describe the human body.

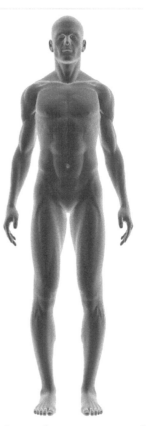

The human body contains approximately 650 muscles, 206 bones, and about 10 pounds of skin. The largest human organ is the skin, with a surface area of about 25 square feet. Each square inch of human skin contains 20 feet of blood vessels. Skin is filled with nerves, which both protect us and give us pleasure. In fact, there are 45 miles of nerves contained in our skin. Not only does it protect our inner organs from evaporation, but it also guards us from the extremes of temperature, harmful rays of sun, infection, and damaging chemicals. It manufactures vitamin D, which turns calcium into bone. This magnificent earth suit can grow or shrink, heal itself, and stretch to allow us freedom of movement. And each and every one of us gets a suit of skin that is totally unique.

Philosophers claim that the essence of a person emanates from the heart. Your heart is a magnificent organ about the size of your clenched fist. It pumps life-sustaining blood through a network of vessels that would be about 60,000 miles long if laid end to end. Your heart works ceaselessly, beating approximately 100,000 times each day. If you live out an average lifespan, your heart will have served you with three billion heartbeats. Your heart supplies your body with fresh oxygen and nutrients and simultaneously clears away harmful waste. Bellows of oxygen are located on either side of your heart for conveniently clearing the blood of carbon dioxide and toxins, then flooding it with oxygen before sending it on another round through the circulatory system. As a protective measure, your heart is cleverly housed in a cage of curved bone.

Your brain consists of 100 billion nerve cells that coordinate thoughts and physical movement, generate emotions, and regulate our unconscious body processes such as digestion, operating internal organs, and breathing. The brain serves as the master control center for the body. It's one of your largest organs and yet weighs only three pounds. Though it makes up only two percent of your total body weight, the brain demands 20 percent of your body's oxygen and calories. Because the brain is extremely delicate, its genius packaging includes three layers of tough membrane called meninges. Each layer is filled with fluid for cushioning. The skull provides a strong, outer shell for the ultimate in protection.

Did you know the muscles in your eyes that help you focus move about 100,000 times each day? Your eyes blink about 15 times a minute or almost 15,000 times while you are awake. And when your eyes close, your brain links information together so you don't even realize they were closed. Simply magnificent!

In order to keep these vital organs and all other tissues of the body functioning efficiently you must provide the cells that comprise the organs with nutrients. The digestive system breaks down food into chemical compounds that are absorbed by every cell. The food you eat travels through 30 feet of intestinal tubing and more than half a dozen organs. When you chew food, it mixes with saliva and enzymes. This starts the process of digestion. After swallowing, digestion becomes involuntary. The food, now called chyme, is mixed with strong 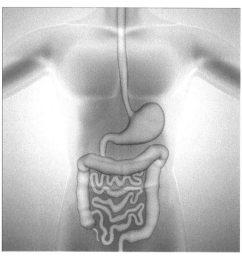 chemicals that break it down further for absorption by cells. Some of these chemicals kill potentially harmful bacteria. As the nutrient mash travels through the digestive system it's processed through key organs such as the liver, gallbladder, and pancreas. The entire journey takes more time than you may imagine. The transit time from eating to elimination averages 53 hours for generally healthy people. That will make you stop and think about your quantity of food.

"Characteristics which define beauty are wholeness, harmony, and radiance." - Thomas Aquinas

Most of us have some knowledge of the science of gastroenterology, or at least know a family member who's been attended by a doctor in that field. Yet, few of us know there is a science of neurogastroenterology. And why should you care? You should care because it is important to know there is a strong correlation between your brain and your gut. This type doctor calls it brain-gut interaction. It has been discovered that a complex nervous system exists inside your gut, which is affectionately known as the enteric nervous system.

Dr. Michael Gershon writes in The Second Brain, that there is, indeed, a brain of sorts in the bowel. Your gut has a greater capacity for "feeling" than does our heart. Have you ever had a "gut feeling" that turned out to be right on target even when circumstantial evidence pointed to a different conclusion? Dr. Gershon has found that there are more nerve cells in our gut than in the entire peripheral nervous system. Serotonin is a hormone that acts as a neurotransmitter. Even though it's manufactured in the brain, 90 percent of our serotonin supply is found in the gut. Serotonin is an important hormone for both the brain and gut as it transmits messages in regard to mood, appetite, sleep, memory and learning, as well as behavior. It also aids in the function of our cardiovascular system and muscles. The gut, which is capable of reflex function independent of the brain, is so much more than a 30 foot tube of digestion machinery! It's in your best interest to develop good habits that keep your sensitive gut happy.

The same guidelines we employ for keeping every other bodily system healthy apply for keeping the gut healthy and functioning properly. Reduce your level of stress and get a regular seven to nine hour a day pattern of sleep. These are key to enjoying the benefits of a healthy gut. Consume nutrient dense foods, food rich in fiber, and drink water. Nutritious foods and water enable the tissues of the gut to function well. Walk regularly to aid circulation and you will make a major contribution toward keeping your system clean. This is the best way to keep the gut relaxed and functioning properly.

Why are these things important for you? All parts of the body interact and integrate as each one relies on the other to function and survive. Without proper care of the magnificent body the grand design breaks down, expected outcomes are diminished, and the natural deterioration that comes with aging is accelerated.

"Excellence is an art won by training and habituation. We do not act rightly because we have virtue or excellence, but we rather have those because we have acted rightly. We are what we repeatedly do. Excellence then, is not an act but a habit." - Aristotle

The Health Project

"The doctor of the future will give no medicine, but will interest his patients in the care of the human frame, in diet, and in the cause and prevention of disease."
- Thomas Edison

The medical community often treats patients with only pharmaceuticals and surgical procedures, ignoring the benefits of preventive methods like eating a clean diet and getting regular exercise. New governmental laws, patient lawsuits, and the additional requirements mandated by insurance agencies have forced changes in how physicians and their staff do business. There is a growing trend toward better health practices that seek to prevent disease and relieve symptoms through proper diet and regular exercise.

Catch the vision Thomas Edison had. Edison saw that the time would come when knowledge regarding "the care of the human frame, diet, and the cause and prevention of disease" would be readily available to us. Our job is to apply this knowledge. Use sound, accurate information for building and maintaining a healthy body. The purpose of this text is to help you take responsibility for the fundamentals of your own good health. Practicing healthful habits may not be easy, but it is simple.

"The quality of a person's life is in direct proportion to their commitment to excellence, regardless of their chosen field of endeavor." - Vincent T. Lombardi

Wikipedia defines health as the level of functional or metabolic efficiency of a living organism. In humans, it is the general condition of our mind and body, usually meaning to be free from illness, injury, or pain. The World Health Organization defines health in its broader sense as "a state of complete physical, mental, and social well-being and not merely the absence of disease or infirmity."

Consider your own level of fitness. Can you climb a flight of stairs with relative ease or does it create a flare of symptoms? How challenging would it be for you to walk a three-mile trail or row a kayak for 20 minutes? And how about the fitness of your mental and social well-being? Mental and social well-being determine emotional health. The condition of your emotional health has a direct impact on your physical health. We will look at ways to relieve stress and get needed rest as we move through the text.

"You were born to win, but to be a winner, you must plan to win, prepare to win, and expect to win." - Zig Ziglar

There are many fitness and weight loss plans and products on the market. Authors and marketers are very crafty in wording the descriptions of their plan to sound as though that particular product or method is the breakthrough discovery that will finally solve the weight and health issues we long to rid ourselves. Don't be frustrated by the gimmicks and tricks. Building strong bodies and minds comes the old fashioned way, by daily practicing the fundamentals of good health.

The first and most basic pillar of health is adequate hydration. Drinking enough water is of paramount importance for overall health. Our bodies are composed of about 70 percent water. Muscle tissue is 75 percent water. Brain and blood cells are more than 80 percent water. Water is the most basic and most important nutrient for your body. Every one of your cells needs water to function properly. Water, and the right kind of fat, makes your cell walls pliable so they take in nutrients and give off waste more efficiently. Water helps your blood flow more easily. When the consistency of blood is optimal, the heart has an easier time pumping it through the circulatory system. Water is the main lubricant for joints. Water is key for proper brain function. If you are feeling sluggish, try drinking a glass of water! It's the nutrient *most* needed for hormone production and the manufacture of neurotransmitters.

Dehydration has many causes. Our bodies lose water through sweat, urine, and our breath. The sun and indoor heat evaporate water from your bodies. Caffeine and salt in our diet also contribute to dehydration. Even a little dehydration can have significant effects that disrupt your health. Dehydration can have a negative impact on important brain functions like short-term memory, visuomotor function and psychomotor functioning. This can impact things like the ability to focus on a computer screen or reading material. Extreme dehydration can cause confusion, disorientation, or the ability to speak or think coherently.

Even though water is acquired through some of the foods you eat, mainly fresh fruit and vegetables, you don't receive as much water as needed through food. To stay hydrated you must be intentional about drinking enough water every day. How much water should you drink in a day? A good formula to follow is to take your body weight in pounds and divide by two. That equals the number of ounces you should drink in a day.

"You are never too old to set another goal or to dream a new dream." - C.S. Lewis

Building Nutritional Habits

Prepare for success. Enrich your life with nutrient dense foods. To have a healthier lifestyle, it's important to give your body what it needs rather than simply satisfying your hunger. The quality of food you consume will determine how well your body functions and for how long. True, natural nutrition is found in living food. Living food comes in a raw, or close to raw state. Living foods contain enzymes, which are active chemicals that aid in breaking down food for digestion. Living food turns brown and decays on your counter within several days. Most packaged foods can last for months without decay because the "life" has been processed out of them.

Fresh fruits and vegetables, whole grains, seeds, and nuts are all living foods. These are foods that are naturally occurring, not manufactured and packaged in a laboratory. Their packaging - skins and peels - is created naturally. The color of the packaging gives clues as to the density of nutrients contained. Take blueberries for instance. They are small dynamos rich in antioxidants – helpful in fighting cancer. They contain many other nutrients including carotenoids, folate, vitamin C, vitamin E, potassium, manganese, magnesium, iron, riboflavin, niacin, and phytoestrogens. These little blue jewels also provide fiber and are low in calories.

"He who takes medicine and neglects diet wastes the skill of his doctors." - Chinese Proverb

Blueberries, and thirteen other foods, are considered to be superfoods. Check out the healthful benefits of these nutrient dense foods.

Superfoods
Beans – help reduce obesity
Blueberries – lower risk for cardiovascular disease
Broccoli – lowers the incidence of cataracts and fights birth defects
Oats – reduce the risk of type II diabetes
Oranges – prevent strokes
Pumpkin – lowers the risk of various cancers
Wild salmon – lowers the risk of heart disease
Soy – lowers cholesterol
Spinach – decreases the chance of cardiovascular disease
Tea – helps prevent osteoporosis
Tomatoes – raise the skin's sun protection factor
Turkey – helps build a strong immune system
Walnuts – reduce the risk of developing coronary heart disease, diabetes, and cancer

Eating living food helps you live a healthful life, enjoying a greater quality of life and the hope for longevity!

The way to develop a more healthful lifestyle is to implement good habits, one choice at a time. By building healthful habits, one step at a time, the process is simplified and tends to become more deeply ingrained in your life than when trying a "quick fix" fad diet. Take an old habit that is not serving you well and replace it with a better one. Try this method for change on a daily basis. Make one change today. Don't look ahead and feel overwhelmed by the idea of radical change.

Focus on the day at hand. You can begin today by taking one simple step toward a clearer mind and healthier body. The following guidelines will lead you in making choices . . . that become habits . . . that develop improved health.

"What you get by achieving your goals is not as important as what you become by achieving your goals."
- Henry David Thoreau

Portion control is a great place to start in making healthful changes. It is ideal to eat small meals frequently throughout the day. Eating this  way helps maintain energy and blood sugar levels. It avoids the spikes and dips in blood sugar that comes with a long period of hunger followed by a large meal. Eating small, frequent portions also helps boost your metabolism because it keeps the digestive system working at an optimal pace.

It is easy to determine portion sizes if you think of it this way. An appropriate portion size for meat is about the size of your fist. Your portion of starchy vegetables or fruit should fit in the palm of one cupped hand. The largest portion should be complex carbohydrates like salad or any variety of green vegetables. A portion of greens should fit into both hands cupped side by side.

Each of your meals should consist of both protein and complex carbohydrates. Carbohydrates give your brain and muscles quick energy. Protein provides amino acids, which are the building blocks for muscle tissue. Because protein is digested more slowly, it keeps you feeling full until the next meal. This carb/protein pairing can be as simple as an apple and a quarter cup of almonds. A small meal, like an apple and nuts, gives you a great energy boost by supplying your body with fiber, the right kind of fat, amino acids, vitamins, and water.

Healthful fats should also be part of each meal. Fat is important for the health of cell membranes, hair, and skin. Consuming fat in your diet helps your body absorb vitamins A, D, E, and K. It is also a vital source of energy. Meat contains fat in varying quantities. Choose lean meats like fish, chicken, turkey, venison, and bison. Because red meat tends to have a higher fat content than other meats and is not as easily digested, it should be eaten with less frequency than other choices. Olive oil, avocados, coconut, seeds, and nuts also provide healthful fats. Aim for 20-30 percent of your daily nutritional intake to come from fat.

Another important habit to develop is maintaining a kitchen stocked with nutritious foods. If good food is readily available, you are more likely to make wise choices. When shopping, focus your attention on foods located on the perimeter of the grocery store. That includes the produce, meat, and dairy sections.

The following is a sample of healthful foods to include as you stock your kitchen. A well-stocked pantry provides a better opportunity for building a healthier you.

Produce

Bananas	Tomatoes
Mushrooms	Apples
Pears	Celery
Raisins	Mixed greens
Spinach	Onions/Purple onion
Cucumbers	Blackberries
Carrots	Red peppers/Green/Orange
Jalapeno peppers	Garlic
Zucchini	Sage (fresh)
Limes/Lemons	Rosemary (fresh)
Radishes	Cilantro
Mint leaves	Baking potatoes/Sweet
Olives	Kiwi
Parsley, fresh	Strawberries
Raspberries	Blueberries
Avocado	Leeks
Broccoli	Asparagus

Dairy

Eggs	Yogurt (low fat/Greek)
Cottage cheese (low fat)	Almond milk/Coconut milk

Grains

Quinoa	Whole-wheat pasta
Rolled oats/Steel cut	Whole-grain cereal
Brown rice	Whole-wheat couscous

Spices

Sea salt	Nutmeg
Cinnamon	Vanilla
Poultry seasoning	Red pepper flakes

Butcher

Skinless chicken	Turkey breast
Sea bass	Lean beef
Salmon fillet	Tilapia

Nuts/Seeds/Beans

Flaxseed	Raw, unsalted almonds
Walnuts	Garbanzo beans
Black beans	Sunflower seeds
Pumpkin seeds	Lentils

Bakery

Ezekiel bread	Sprouted grains
Whole-wheat wraps	Brown rice cakes

Choose the organic version for some food. The Dirty Dozen is a list of fruits and vegetables that are more easily contaminated by pesticides because their thin skin provides little protection. Choose organic for these when possible:

Apples	Peaches	Grapes
Bell peppers	Pears	Nectarines
Celery	Potatoes	Spinach
Cherries	Raspberries	Strawberries

Congratulations! You are moving forward in your quest for a stronger, leaner, more energetic you. You are eating small portions of nutrient rich foods periodically through the day. And this one habit alone is giving you more energy and a brighter outlook. Now, your pantry and refrigerator are stocked with nutritious foods. What's next?

Prepare meals at home. The key here is control. You have control over what ingredients are used, the quality of the ingredients, portion sizes, and the cleanliness of the prep area. Preparing meals at home reduces your food budget. When you eat at home, there's less time spent deciding where to dine, driving there, and waiting for service.

"It's not what you know, but what you use that makes a difference." - Zig Ziglar

There are many resources online and in stores to guide you in the simple preparation of meals at home. This is beneficial for you and your family in many ways. The kitchen is a cozy spot for working together as a family as you discuss the events of the day. Allow children to participate in preparing the meal and setting the table. It gives them a sense of accomplishment and teamwork. Working together in the home builds a bond of loyalty within the family unit. Make it a lighthearted environment where creativity and individual contribution are enjoyed.

"A crust eaten in peace is better than a banquet partaken in anxiety." - Aesop's Fables

You will enjoy meal prep if you keep it simple. On your day off, bake a pan of chicken and a pan of potatoes. Store those in the refrigerator to use in meals during the week. Prepare a tossed salad and store in an airtight container. The slow cooker, or crockpot, is a very helpful tool. Before going to work, drop a roast, cut potatoes, and carrots in on the low setting, add beef broth and seasonings. Ahhh . . . the aroma of a hot, delicious meal greets you at the door when you return home.

Have the kids set the table and use their imaginations to decorate it. There are many helpful websites and blogs filled with family meal ideas and recipes. Relaxing background music helps busy minds relax which aids digestion. Everyone will be thankful to share a quiet evening at home around the dinner table. Studies show that people who eat home-cooked meals on a regular basis have more control over weight management and enjoy stronger immune systems.

"Mirth is God's medicine. Everybody ought to bathe in it."
- Henry Ward Beecher

Let's look at another habit you can develop to help you eat properly during the day. Pack a cooler to take along so you have good choices at work or while running errands. Purchase small storage containers from the grocery or discount store. You can pack leftovers from the dinner you prepared earlier in the week. Mix oatmeal with chopped walnuts and blueberries for a filling treat. Pack a couple of pieces of fruit. Add protein to your cooler stash by packing nuts, seeds, or garbanzo beans. Crackers with peanut butter make a good quick snack. Tuna and salmon can be purchased in pouches, which make them very easy to carry along.

Finally, always carry plenty of pure water. Adding lemon or lime juice to the water makes it especially refreshing. Good hydration is fundamental to weight control.

Look at the progress you are making:

Eating smaller portions
Keeping your energy levels up with frequent meals
Making nutritious food available in your home
Exploring creative ways to enjoy simple, home cooked meals
Finally, you are carrying good food and water with you as you travel away from home

What great habits! Not only will your health improve with these consistent efforts, but also those around you will begin to notice the changes and be positively influenced to begin making similar changes.

The best six doctors anywhere
and no one can deny it
are sunshine, water, rest, and air
exercise and diet.
These six will gladly you attend
if only you are willing.
Your mind they'll ease
your will they'll mend
and charge you not a shilling.

Nursery rhyme quoted by Wayne Fields, *What the River Knows*, 1990

Empower Yourself
Read Those Labels!

Learning how to read a nutrition label is a fundamental skill for making smarter nutrition choices. Processed foods are required by law to contain a package label describing the serving size, how many servings are in a package, and basic nutrition information related to calories, protein, fat, sugars, fiber, vitamins, minerals and other nutrients. In addition, processed foods also contain an ingredient list. Together, this information is supposed to help a consumer make an informed decision. But the process of actually doing this is complicated. Here are some tips on how to read and understand the nutrition label. After reading, I think you will agree that we need an easier way to determine if a food is "healthier" or not.

- **Start from the top with the serving size and the number of servings per container**. All of the nutrient amounts listed on the food label are for one serving, so it is important to determine how many servings are actually being consumed to accurately assess nutrient intake.
- **Look at the total calories**. This part of the nutrition label is the most important factor for weight control. In general, 40 calories per serving is considered low, 100 calories is moderate, and 400 or more calories is considered high.
- **The next two sections of the label note the nutrient content of the food product**. Try to minimize intake of saturated and trans fat, cholesterol, and sodium—and aim to consume adequate amounts of vitamins and minerals, especially fiber, vitamin A, vitamin C, calcium and iron. The food label includes the total amount of sugars (natural and added). Though the label does not separately identify added sugars, natural sugars are found in milk, fruit and other ingredients. Therefore, if the food item does not belong to those food groups, the amount of sugar contained in the product approximates added sugar. For foods that contain milk or fruit, added sugars can be identified in the ingredients list.
- **Review percent daily values (PDV).** The footnote at the bottom of the label reminds consumers that all PDVs are based on a 2,000-calorie diet. If you need more or fewer calories, adjust recommendations accordingly. For example, three grams of fat provides five percent of the recommended amount for someone on a 2,000-calorie diet, but seven percent for someone on a 1,500-calorie diet. The footnote also includes daily values for nutrients you should limit (saturated fat, trans fat, cholesterol, and sodium), recommended carbohydrate intake for a 2,000-

calorie diet (60 percent of calories), and minimal fiber recommendations for 2,000- and 2,500-calorie diets. This site provides information on determining your calorie needs: supertracker.usda.gov.

- **Check for allergens.** Legislation also requires food manufacturers to list all potential food allergens on food packaging. The most common food allergens are fish, shellfish, soybean, wheat, egg, milk, peanuts and tree nuts. This information is usually included near the list of ingredients on the package. For those who follow a gluten-free diet, this is also an easy way to identify if wheat is a product ingredient.
- **Carefully review the ingredients list.** Note that the ingredient list is in decreasing order of substance weight in the product. That is, the ingredients that are listed first are the most abundant in the product. The ingredient list is useful for identifying whether or not the product contains trans fat, solid fats, added sugars, whole grains and refined grains. Note that although trans-fat is included in the "fat" section of the nutrition label, if the product contains <0.5g per serving, the manufacturer does not need to claim it. However, if a product contains partially hydrogenated oils, then the product contains trans fat and should be avoided.
- **Solid fats:** If the ingredient list contains beef fat, butter, chicken fat, coconut oil, cream, hydrogenated oils, palm kernel oils, pork fat, shortening or stick margarine, then the product contains solid fats. The Dietary Guidelines advise limiting solid fats.
- **Added sugars:** Ingredients signifying added sugars include anhydrous dextrose, brown sugar, confectioner's powdered sugar, corn syrup, corn syrup solids, dextrin,

fructose, high-fructose corn syrup, honey, invert sugar, lactose, malt syrup, maltose, maple syrup, molasses, nectar, pancake syrup, raw sugar, sucrose, sugar, white granulated sugar, cane juice, evaporated corn sweetener, fruit juice concentrate, crystal dextrose, glucose, liquid fructose, sugar cane juice and fruit nectar. In many cases, products contain multiple forms of sugar.

- **Whole grains:** If whole grains are the primary ingredient, then the product is 100 percent whole grain. The whole grain should be the first or second ingredient. Examples of whole grains include brown rice, buckwheat, bulgur (cracked wheat), millet, oatmeal, popcorn, quinoa, rolled oats, whole-grain sorghum, whole-grain triticale, whole-grain barley, whole-grain corn, whole oats/oatmeal, whole rye, whole wheat and wild rice.
- **Refined grains:** Refined grains should be "enriched." If the first ingredient is an **enriched** grain, then the product is not a whole grain. This is one way to understand whether or not a "wheat bread" is actually whole wheat or a refined product.

While the food label is found on the side or the back of products, other health and nutrition claims are often visibly displayed on the front of the package. Though the FDA regulates these claims, they are frequently a source of confusion. You should be skeptical of front-of-package claims and evaluate them on a case-by-case basis. A loophole allowing **qualified health claims** has paved the way for manufacturers to claim unproven benefits to products, as long as the label states the claim is supported by very little scientific evidence.

This process of trying to make sense of food labels to make healthy choices is complex. In an attempt to simplify the process, many efforts have been made to create easier-to-understand labels but none have become standard. With the technological advances and the widespread use of smartphones, several apps are now on the market that can help to simplify the process of making healthy nutrition choices. For example, www.fooducate.com allows you to scan the bar code of a processed food and the app will give the food a grade A-D, based on its nutritional value.

Maybe one day it won't be so hard, but for now, whether you use an app for help or do the analysis yourself, it pays to know how to use food labels to make smarter choices.

Get Moving!

Have you ever seen a stagnant pond? On my grandfather's farm in the fall, beavers worked tirelessly gnawing down small trees, stacking them in the water, then securing the structure with mud and rocks to create an underwater home. On more than one occasion, my grandfather bought sticks of dynamite and destroyed these watery castles because they were blocking the flow of water through his pond. This blast was required because when the flow of water stopped, toxins and algae accumulated. Green sludge covered the perimeter of the pond and created a potentially toxic environment. There was a fish kill one year when he didn't get to the "blow-it-up-yourself" store in time. Many fish died and floated to the surface of the pond. As a child, I was alarmed to see the effects of the stagnant water as I looked on at the floating, belly-up carcasses and smelled the stench rising from the surface of the water. It was one big, stinky mess!

When water is flowing in a river or stream, life thrives. Waterfalls and rivers are beautiful, teaming with life. Rocks in rivers filter water in the same way your kidneys and liver filter blood as it flows through the circulatory system. If you want to clear your body of toxins and waste, refresh yourself with movement. A simple ten minute walk can refresh your mind, heart, and lungs. Your body is designed for movement and thrives with daily use. Stagnant ponds and stagnant bodies become a breeding ground for disease. So, lace up those shoes and get moving!

"Do not think of today's failures, but of the success that may come tomorrow. You have set yourselves a difficult task, but you will succeed if you persevere." - Helen Keller

Many studies have shown that exercise has a powerful effect on health. <u>The Journal of the American Medical Association</u> found that women who walked briskly for at least two hours per week reduced their risk of developing breast cancer. By increasing the rate of circulation of blood and oxygen, toxins can be collected and removed from cells more efficiently. They are then expelled from the body through sweat glands, urine, and exhalation. Exercise has an internal cleansing effect.

Did you know that regular exercise can lower your heart rate? This is a good thing! The active person's heart is better conditioned and works more efficiently than the heart of one who remains sedentary. The well-conditioned heart beats

fewer times per minute, working more efficiently. Conditioning your heart through regular exercise increases your chances for enjoying a long, healthy life. Exercise also conditions the coronary arteries, which improves blood flow. As you can see, daily movement can certainly reduce your risk of disease.

Cardiovascular exercise is the key to keeping your organs and systems of the body functioning efficiently. It is easy to see how movement positively affects the circulatory and respiratory systems.

Exercise increases the rate of perspiration. Have you worked up a good sweat  lately? Your skin serves you by releasing toxins and waste through sweat. When your body moves briskly, your heart rate and circulation increase. As blood circulates, it picks up waste from cells and organs. Perspiration washes out waste and helps maintain body temperature.

Your lymphatic system also does its job more efficiently when the body is actively building muscle through resistance exercise. The lymphatic system is responsible for clearing out bacteria, viruses, and toxins. This powerhouse cleaning system operates by muscle contraction rather than blood flow. When muscles remain stagnant, the lymphatic system can't "clean house" as thoroughly as when muscles are being challenged with resistance training exercises.

Strength, or resistance, training increases muscle mass. Muscle is highly metabolic tissue. The more muscle you possess, the more calories you burn in an hour, even at rest. Muscle tissue is lost through degeneration as we age. By the time you celebrate your 30th birthday, your body is losing about one half pound of lean muscle tissue a year. Unless you are intentional about building muscle tissue, that loss accelerates with age, especially if you live a sedentary lifestyle. Resistance training also serves to build bone density, protecting the body from osteoporosis. Research suggests that exercise works better than calcium to build strong bones. Strength training helps improve posture. Strong muscles give better support for joints, reducing your risk of injury. Through weight training you will improve your balance and core strength. One of the most appealing affects of weight training is the youthful appearance developed by building shapely muscles. What a great side effect! Another important component that must not be overlooked while building a sturdy frame is maintaining or developing flexibility. As you exercise, muscle tissue swells with blood and fluids. It is imperative to cool down with slower walking followed by stretching to prevent pooling of this fluid in your joints. Stretching also serves to keep muscle tissue pliable as it builds in density and strength, protecting connecting joints.

If your job keeps you posted at a desk for long periods of time, get up and move through a range of motions that stretch the major muscle groups. March in place for a minute. This will increase blood flow bringing a refreshing wave of oxygen and nutrients to your brain and muscles. Set your phone to ping at the top of the hour, reminding you it is time for a stretch break. Even 60 seconds of movement per hour makes a big contribution toward reversing the negative effects of a sedentary lifestyle.

There are many guides available for learning various forms of exercise. The choices can be overwhelming! In an effort to build exercise into your life and make it part of your lifestyle, begin with something you know. Start with something simple like walking. Walking outdoors not only burns calories and fat, it is ideal for strengthening all systems of the body, especially the cardiovascular and respiratory systems. Walking outside refreshes  your body and your mind. With oxygen and blood flow refreshing the brain, new ideas and solutions appear. Walking can have a tremendous restoring and cleansing effect mentally as well as physically. It is free. It is enjoyable. It adds value to your life.

"Your goals are the roadmaps that guide you and show you what is possible for your life." - Les Brown

When you progress to more advanced activities, make sure you receive proper instruction to reduce your risk of injury. The American Council on Exercise has a website containing basic information on proper exercise and diet. Use trusted resources and professionals to guide you as you begin an exercise program or participate in sporting activities.

A good way to begin building strength through regular exercise is to start slowly and build gradually. Give equal attention to all major muscle groups in order to keep connecting joints free from strain. Practice flexibility exercises to cool down and relax. Flexibility is important for maintaining a comfortable range of motion as muscle tissue increases in size and density.

Finally, participate in activities that you find challenging and fun! Play ball with your kids. Take a walk on the beach or through the zoo. Hula hoop! Join a tennis team. Swim laps at the YMCA. Ride bikes. Enroll for dance lessons. Set up a ping pong table and call a few friends over . . . you will improve your health, and theirs, while bringing out the laughs.

"What soap is to the body, laughter is to the soul."
- Yiddish Proverb

Stress Reduction Practices

Exercise goes a long way in reducing stress and its negative side effects. Proper nutrition also helps keep your mental and physical being sharp and strong. In addition, there are many other things you can do to reduce stress in your life.

Make it your goal to practice mindfulness – pay attention to the events of the moment rather than running ahead to the worries of tomorrow. A friend once advised me, "Wherever you are, be there." Focus your energy on what you can do today to be well. Keep a written list of tasks that must be accomplished. That helps free brain space and allows you to keep your attention on the task at hand. When tomorrow comes, you will again focus your attention on the tasks for that day. Living in the present and making the most of the day is a good habit to relieve stressful thoughts and accomplish what needs to be done.

"Therefore do not worry about tomorrow, for tomorrow will worry about itself. Each day has enough trouble of its own." - Matthew 6:34

Mindfulness finds ways to enjoy the present. As you drive, enjoy the beautiful scenery around you. Listen to encouraging music and speakers as you drive or work around home. When cooking dinner, savor the smells and tastes. Practice thankfulness. Allow yourself to enjoy this moment that you are in. Begin replacing negative thoughts with more positive ones by naming things you are thankful for. There are many people in the world that would love to have your job, your car, your home, and your choices. Have you made a list of your blessings lately? Take a few minutes today to write them down. The attitude of gratitude goes a long way toward diminishing troublesome thoughts.

"Where your focus goes, your energy flows." - Les Brown

You may have heard that laughter is the best medicine. And indeed, when you laugh powerful chemicals called endorphins are released in your brain. Endorphins act much like morphine as they relieve pain, and relax your body.  Laughing lowers the level of stress hormones, boosts the immune system, and brightens the dark cloud of depression. That's reason enough to read a funny book before bedtime. It may help you relax and sleep more soundly.

"When people are laughing, they're generally not killing each other." - Alan Alda

There are simple things like practicing thankfulness and looking for humor that are within your control. Other things are outside your control and can create tremendous stress like accidents, illness, death of a loved one, or loss of a job. Be prepared as much as possible by having your affairs in order before trouble comes. Know the resources available to you and where to go for assistance. Ask for help when needed. Everyone wins when we bear each other's burdens.

A very wise teacher once told me that our thoughts determine our feelings. Our thoughts and feelings together determine the decisions we make. This process goes on in the mind, unseen to the rest of the world. The decisions, then, determine the behaviors. Behavior is the outward expression of this mental course of action. All behavior originates with the thoughts you allow your mind to dwell on.

"Change your thoughts, change your life." - Lao Tzu

Principles of Positive Thinking

1. Your thoughts have power over your feelings and attitudes.
2. You can change yourself by changing your thoughts.
3. Positive thinkers use faith to gain control of problems.
4. Fear and worry are conquered by practical spiritual methods; meditation and prayer increase vitality and peace of mind.
5. A positive mind leads to improved health and well-being.
6. Positive thinkers overcome mistakes, forgiving themselves and others.
7. The practice of positive imaging instills the courage and confidence to achieve goals.
8. Enthusiasm leads to action.
9. Positive attitudes create more enduring and fulfilling relationships.
10. Positive thinking is achievable by all people.

Sleep Enough

Sleep is a critical component to maintaining a healthy body. While you sleep, your body goes through a process of cleaning, rebuilding, healing, and restoring. New cells replace old ones. Your immune system is recharged. Thoughts are organized in your mind. When you give yourself proper rest, mental and physical health is maintained. The best medicine for a sick or injured person is simply rest. Proper rest allows your immune system to heal your body naturally.

Hormones are regulated during sleep. For your adrenal glands to function properly, and produce the needed hormones, plenty of sleep is required. Two of these hormones, growth hormone and leptin, are secreted during sleep cycles and are responsible for building tissue and maintaining a healthy weight. Conversely, stress and a deficit of sleep can raise levels of the hormone cortisol. There are other factors that contribute to high cortisol levels – recent illness, injury, or surgery. These are usually temporary situations and with rest and healing the levels will return to normal. High levels of cortisol, sustained over long periods of time, have been known to increase belly fat and reduce sex drive. Elevated cortisol levels are also associated with conditions like depression, obesity, and disease of the liver or kidneys. Getting eight hours of sleep helps reduce cortisol levels, which means a reduced risk of symptoms and disease.

"Take rest; a field that has rested gives a bountiful crop."
-Ovid

Another serious risk you incur if you keep a running tab of sleep deprivation is that of developing type II diabetes. Because a lack of sleep impairs your body's natural ability to digest and distribute food properly, you put yourself at greater risk of developing this disease. There are other diseases directly associated with sleep deprivation such as chronic fatigue syndrome, hypertension, depression, and fibromyalgia.

You have heard it said, "Work hard. Play hard." That sounds like a good way to bring balance to your life, but in fact, the healthful way to balance hard work is with rest. Certainly, recreation is an enjoyable part of rest, but a full eight hours of sleep is the more necessary component of balancing out a day of hard work. Make sleep a priority. How well you sleep is one of the major factors in predicting longevity. A good night's sleep actually helps you live longer.

There are a number of ways to be intentional about getting the sleep your body needs to function optimally. Prepare your bedroom by cleaning and organizing so it has a calm, peaceful look and feel. Cover the windows with blinds or black out shades to make the room dark. Avoid using electronic devices thirty minutes before retiring to bed. The light used in these devises can be stimulating to your brain. End your consumption of caffeinated food and drinks, alcohol, and heavy meals at least a couple of hours prior to bedtime. A brisk walk helps your body relax better during sleep, but be sure to finish your exercise a couple of hours before settling in since exercise raises your heart rate and increases alertness temporarily. Allow your body to relax gradually as you prepare for sleep.

Many people find it relaxing to read as a means of calming their mind. If you have trouble relaxing because of your to-do list, jot the list down on paper so you have it available to deal with during waking hours. A glass of milk or warm, herbal tea (decaf) can be very helpful in relaxing your mind and body. Find the steps that help you most and create a habit of preparing for a good night's sleep.

Meeting the Challenges of Shift Work

My friend has a new Ferrari. What a beautiful machine! It is much faster than he could possibly need in our small, congested town, but it is the finest car I've ever seen. You can be sure he uses only the highest grade fuel and oil to maintain it. How much more imperative is it that you use quality care for the magnificent vehicle that is *you*! Your body is infinitely more complex and valuable than anything made by human hands. When given good nutrition, exercise, and rest, your body will serve you well. Your body is the vehicle that controls the control room. How important is it that you care properly for it so it can perform its duty with ease?

Best nutrition practices were mentioned at length in a previous chapter, but shiftwork presents a unique need for taking the planning process a step further. Because your metabolism naturally slows down late in the day and into the night, it is important to be purposeful about choosing food that helps you stay alert and energized. Eat nutritious food about every three hours to keep your body fueled with energy. Keep portions small. Heavy meals can make you sleepy because blood becomes concentrated on the digestion process and is therefore drawn away from the brain and other organs. This may leave you feeling cold and sleepy. Combine a protein rich food with complex carbohydrates. Avoid sugary and processed foods as these can cause a spike in blood sugar levels followed by a drop that can leave you feeling drowsy. Drink plenty of water to hydrate your brain. This simple action step goes a long way toward helping you stay alert.

One of the nutritional habits previously discussed is packing a cooler to carry good food with you. This is a great practice for work, whether working day or night shift. Preparing and packing your own food gives you control over the fuel you take to strengthen your body. Leftover meat and veggies are always a good choice for the cooler. A small container of natural peanut butter and a banana make a good combination of protein and complex carbs. Spicy hummus and baby carrots pack a punch for the taste buds and satisfy nutritional needs. Avoid packing simple carbs like cookies, chips, sodas, and similar food imposters that add calories and fat with no nutritional benefits. In addition, simple carbs make you feel sleepy.

Here are some other suggestions for packing your cooler:

- Mixture of nuts, pumpkin seeds, sunflower seeds, and chopped dried fruit
- Lean meat with cheese, lettuce, avocado rolled in a tortilla with dressing or salsa for dipping
- Oatmeal packet, add nuts and fruit
- Tuna and pickles with crackers
- Apple or banana and nut butter
- Yogurt mixed with fruit, nuts, seeds, and/or granola
- Veggie variety and hummus
- Baked potato and a cup of chili
- Instant grits, hard-boiled egg and sausage links
- Soup and a sandwich

Your final meal before the end of your shift should include meat like turkey, chicken, or lean beef. Meat contains building blocks called amino acids. One of these amino acids, tryptophan, is key for making the hormone serotonin in the brain. Serotonin is not only important for brain function but is a natural sleep aid. Have you ever fallen asleep on the sofa after a turkey dinner? Most of us have. Turkey is a rich source of tryptophan and is healthful, lean meat. The last meal of your shift should contain a portion of lean meat. Because protein takes longer than carbs to be broken down, you will feel full longer allowing you to sleep without hunger pains. Also, the tryptophan will help you relax and fall asleep more easily. As the end of your shift nears, end consumption of food and drink giving your body time to digest the fuel so you can begin balancing out your day with rest.

Sleep is governed by two regulating body systems: the circadian biological clock and sleep/wake homeostasis. The circadian rhythm tells your body when to sleep. There are natural dips and rises in wakefulness in a 24 hour period. The strongest drive to sleep occurs between 2:00-4:00 a.m. and 1:00-3:00 p.m. If you haven't had enough sleep the day before, you may feel more compelled to nap during these dips in energy levels. If permissible, take turns with your work partner to nap briefly. Even a 15-20 minute rest goes a long way in refreshing tired eyes.

Sleep/wake homeostasis tells us that a need for sleep is accumulating and it is time to go to sleep. This is referred to as sleep debt. All debts must be paid and the only way to pay off this one is with quality sleep. Sleep/wake homeostasis is our body's system for maintaining balance between energy spent and energy restored.

How necessary is sleep? Randy Gardner, a 17-year-old high school student from San Diego, stayed awake for eleven straight days. He felt nauseous at times, had difficulty reading, suffered temporary memory lapses, and experienced feelings of paranoia during the experiment. This scientifically monitored look into the need for sleep provides documentation on the longest period of time anyone has gone without sleep. While scores of people have gone without food for weeks, no one survives long without sleep.

Shift workers may have more difficulty getting the necessary eight hours of sleep in a day. The shifts may be long in duration creating more difficulty relaxing for deep sleep. Your circadian rhythms can be disrupted due to shiftwork. Those who work this type schedule know all too well the physical complications that result. A sleep-deprived body doesn't produce insulin as effectively which can lead to type II diabetes. Sleep deprivation means energy deprivation and it is easy to reach for food to try to meet the need for energy. This, of course, can lead to unwanted, excess weight.

Often, the psychological complications can be more challenging to overcome. When you are overly fatigued, memory and cognitive function are compromised. Irritability can affect your mood and responses. Long durations of fatigue can even lead to depression.

"Laughter is an instant vacation." - Milton Berle

There are specific steps you can take to help get the rest you need. A good first step is to talk with your doctor if you are unable to sleep soundly due to physical problems like excessive snoring, cramping or restlessness in your legs, and even periods of wakefulness due to digestive distress or difficulty breathing. Sleep disorders and digestive issues can disrupt sleep, causing fatigue to accumulate. Over time, this sleep debt can lead to serious health problems and create greater risk for accidents at home and on the job.

Prepare in advance for a restful sleep by enlisting the understanding and support of family and friends. Describe the unique challenges you face as a shift worker and ask them to support you in getting adequate rest and recovery. Many find it helpful to post their work and sleep schedule on a calendar that hangs in a common area where all family members can see. Other activities can then be added to the calendar so the family and shift worker can coordinate the details of each month. When everyone knows what to expect, conflict is diminished. It may also help to hang a "do not disturb" notice on the bedroom door while you are sleeping. That serves to remind others not to enter the room, allowing you to sleep without interruption.

Those who sleep during the day must be more intentional about getting the sleep they need. When leaving the nightshift, the sun may be rising. Natural light is a cue for your body to wake. Therefore, you need to do everything you can to block out increasingly bright light. Put on sunglasses before stepping outside to drive home. Keep light to a minimum once reaching home and while preparing for bed. Install black out shades or curtains to prevent light from entering the room. Wear a sleep mask to block any remaining light. Lower the temperature in the room so your body can fully relax rather than struggle due to overheating. Have a fan or sound machine running to drown out surrounding noises. There are free sound machine apps to download on your phone or tablet that provide a variety of white noise and ambient sounds. Turn off distractions such as ringers and televisions. Remember to plug in your electronic devices before falling asleep because those batteries need recharging too.

Making Change

For you to live a healthful lifestyle you must first answer the question, "Do you want to be well?" It seems the obvious answer is "yes, of course!" But do you really want to be well, *really*? Most everyone would agree that to be strong, fit, and free of disease is the better way to live. But, because we live in a polluted environment and live sedentary lives, healthy bodies don't happen without intentional effort. Steps must be taken daily in order to develop the kind of habits that create a healthy life.

Change doesn't come easily for most of us. Humans tend to prefer the familiar. We gravitate toward our own personal comfort zone and prefer to snuggle in and stay there. Implementing new habits that move us away from known comfort can feel overwhelming.

"Faith is taking the first step even when you don't see the whole staircase." - Martin Luther King, Jr.

The most effective method for building new habits is to make small changes over time. Start with something doable. If you want to exercise but haven't done any in a long time you might begin to change by marching in place while watching TV for a few minutes a day. When that starts to become easier, add five minutes. The key is to take action and continue it on a consistent basis.

Making change in a step-by-step process like this is called the kaizen method. Kaizen's small change concept helps avoid the fear that's often associated with turning in a new direction.

"A journey of a thousand miles must begin with the first step." - Lao Tzu

Psychologist James Prochaska had a strong desire to help people make change by breaking bad habits and developing habits that bought them renewed vitality. After watching his alcoholic father die, helping people change for the better became a driving passion. He studied people who had made successful, lasting change in order to discover the method they used. Most all of them had progressed through the same six stages.

He found the biggest key to success is never giving up!

Prochaska's Transtheoretical Model

Stage 1
Pre-contemplation – you know what you need to do, but aren't sure you want to
Strategy – list the pros and cons

Stage 2
Contemplation – you are considering change, but not yet ready to take action
Strategy – list the pros and cons

Stage 3
Preparation – you have decided to change and take action soon
Strategy – write goals: initial short term/long term; enlist the support of family and friends

Stage 4
Action – begin to move/"Just do it!"
Strategy – post positive notes and your workout schedule

Stage 5
Maintenance – you begin enjoying the benefits of your new habit
Strategy – visualize yourself in this new place/learn from mistakes/continue improving

Stage 6
Termination – you have terminated the old and have replaced it with the new
Strategy – congratulate yourself/help someone else make change

Use the kaizen method by taking small, continuous steps that lead to change. Maybe you begin by drinking a bottle of water in the morning. Another good place to begin is reducing the size of your portions at mealtime. Start with one thing until it becomes your new habit.

Making change with small steps helps you feel more comfortable about a different behavior. Once you get the hang of a small change, begin another. When you continue that path without giving up, your outcomes look and feel different.

Use the next graphic to guide you in making positive changes to address the health and fitness challenges you face. Finally, the poem "Don't Quit," by Edgar Guest, has been instrumental in motivating me and many others. Post it and refer to it often for encouragement.

Celebrate
your success.

Savor the benefits.

Build as you go.

Remain consistent.

Continue with small action steps.

Begin to move.

Start small.

Choose an action.

Don't Quit

When things go wrong, as they sometimes will,
When the road you're trudging seems all up hill,
When the funds are low and the debts are high,
And you want to smile, but you have to sigh,
When care is pressing you down a bit,
Rest! if you must; but don't you quit.

Life is queer with its twist and turns,
As everyone of us sometimes learns,
And many a failure turns about
When he might have won had he stuck it out;
Don't give up, though the pace seems slow;
You might succeed with another blow.

Often the goal is nearer than
It seems to a faint and faltering man,
Often the struggler has given up
When he might have captured the victor's cup.
And he learned too late, when the night slipped down,
How close he was to the golden crown.

Success is failure turned inside out;
The silver tint of the clouds of doubt;
And you never can tell how close you are,
It may be near when it seems afar;
So stick to the fight when you're hardest hit;
It's when things seem worst that you mustn't quit.

- Edgar Guest

Conclusion

You are a magnificent human! Are you making the most of the life you have been given? Life can get so hectic with daily responsibilities and interruptions that you don't take time to consider the path you are on and where it is leading you. As the years roll on, the need to be intentional about taking care of yourself increases. Working in a safety-critical job also creates a need for an extra measure of self-care.

Take time to step back and think, truly reflect on your life, the people you care about, your work, and your home. What's important to you? Chances are if you take better care of yourself, you will be a better spouse, parent, friend, and employee.

Why might you change? Pick a number on a scale from 1 to 10 with 1 meaning "I am not ready for change" to 10 meaning "I'm totally ready, bring on change!" Now, you are thinking of a number. If you chose a 2 or higher, you are indicating that you do see a need for change. You do recognize some aspect that needs improving. What small step can you take today to move forward in that one area of your life? Visualize yourself with change already happening. If you made a change, what might the outcome be? Why is this outcome important to you?

Take a few minutes to think through these questions. Write down your answers. Seeing your answers in black and white will bring out a whole new level of awareness. The first step will become evident as you look over your answers. Begin change with the first step. The first step is always the hardest. If you need a push, review your reasons for making a change. Simply starting helps remove the barrier created by the fear of change. Start today and don't ever, ever quit!

References

www.who.int/about/definition definition of health, 10 January 2015

www.en.wiki/health.org definition of health, 24 January 2015

Gershon, Michael. The Second Brain. Harper Perennial. 11-17-1999

www.bls.gov/cps. Bureau of Labor Statistics, 21 February 2015

www.foodnews.org Dirty Dozen, 28 February 2105

www.jama.jamanetwork.com Breast Cancer and Exercise, 28 February 2015

Peale, Norman Vincent. ISBN-13: 9780671764708. Simon & Schuster. 28 August 1987

www.scientificamerican.com Need for Sleep, 7 March 2015

www.danddteamtraining.com Don't Quit, 2 September 2015

www.wikipedia.org Edgar Albert Guest, 5 September 2015